TAHITI & FRENCH POLYNESIA

TRAVEL GUIDE 2025 –2026

Your Ultimate Companion to explore the Hidden Gems and Attractions.

Isabelle M. Fry

Tahiti & French Polynesia Travel Guide 2025-2026

Isabelle M. Fry

Copyright © 2025 by Isabelle M. Fry

All rights reserved.

No part of this publication may be reproduced, distributed, or transmitted in any form or by any means, including photocopying, recording, or other electronic or mechanical methods, without the prior written permission of the publisher, except in the case of brief quotations embodied in critical reviews and certain other non-commercial uses permitted by copyright law.

DISCLAIMER

This travel guide is provided for informational purposes only. The information contained herein is believed to be accurate and reliable as of the publication date, but may be subject to change. We are not making any warranty, express or implied, with respect to the content of this guide.

Users of this guide are responsible for verifying information independently and consulting appropriate authorities and resources prior to travel. We are not liable for any loss or damage caused by the reliance on information contained in this guide.

Information regarding travel advisories, visas, health, safety, and other important considerations can change rapidly. Users are advised to check for the most up-to-date information from official government and travel industry sources before embarking on any trip.

Travel inherently involves risk, and users are responsible for making their own informed decisions and accepting any associated risks.

Isabelle M. Fry

TABLE OF CONTENTS

INTRODUCTION 9
CHAPTER 1 11
   WELCOME TO TAHITI & FRENCH POLYNESIA 11
   WHY VISIT TAHITI & FRENCH POLYNESIA? 11
   HOW TO USE THIS GUIDE 13
CHAPTER 2 15
   GETTING THERE 15
   FLIGHTS AND AIRLINES 15
   VISA AND ENTRY REQUIREMENTS 16
   TRANSPORTATION OPTIONS 17
CHAPTER 3 19
   ACCOMMODATION 19
   LUXURY RESORTS 19
   BOUTIQUE HOTELS 20
   BUDGET-FRIENDLY STAYS 21
   OVERWATER BUNGALOWS: THE ULTIMATE EXPERIENCE 22
CHAPTER 4 25
   GETTING AROUND 25
   PUBLIC TRANSPORTATION 25
CHAPTER 5 29
   MUST-SEE ATTRACTIONS 29
   NATURAL WONDERS: LAGOONS, MOUNTAINS, AND WATERFALLS 29
   BEACHES: BEST SPOTS FOR SUN, SAND, AND SURF 30
   HISTORICAL SITES AND MUSEUMS 31
CHAPTER 6 35
   FOOD AND DRINK 35
   MUST-TRY DISHES 36
   BEST RESTAURANTS AND LOCAL EATERIES 37
CHAPTER 7 41
   CULTURE AND CUSTOMS 41
   LANGUAGE AND COMMUNICATION 46
CHAPTER 8 47
   LAWS AND GUIDELINES 47
   IMPORTANT LAWS FOR VISITORS 47
   SAFETY TIPS AND PRECAUTIONS 49
CHAPTER 9 53
   MONEY MATTERS 53

PRACTICAL TIPS FOR MANAGING MONEY	55
CHAPTER 10	**57**
PRACTICAL TIPS	57
PACKING LIST AND TRAVEL ESSENTIALS	57
CLIMATE AND WEATHER: BEST TIME TO VISIT	59
CONNECTIVITY: INTERNET AND PHONE SERVICES	60
CHAPTER 11	**63**
DAY TRIPS AND EXCURSIONS	63
NEIGHBORING ISLANDS: MUST-VISIT DESTINATIONS	63
GUIDED TOURS AND ACTIVITIES	64
DIY ADVENTURE TIPS	65
CHAPTER 12	**67**
SHOPPING AND SOUVENIRS	67
BEST MARKETS AND SHOPS	67
WHAT TO BUY	68
CHAPTER 13	**71**
SPECIAL INTERESTS	71
HONEYMOON AND ROMANTIC GETAWAYS	71
FAMILY-FRIENDLY ACTIVITIES	72
SOLO TRAVEL TIPS	73
WELLNESS AND SPA RETREATS	75
CHAPTER 14	**77**
FINAL TRAVEL TIPS	77
STAYING CONNECTED AND KEEPING MEMORIES	78
PLAN YOUR RETURN TRIP	79
CHAPTER 15	**81**
PREPARING FOR YOUR TRIP	81
PRE-TRIP PLANNING AND RESEARCH	81
BUDGETING AND FINANCIAL PLANNING	82
TECHNOLOGY AND CONNECTIVITY	85
CONCLUSION	**87**
BONUS	**89**
TRAVEL PLANNER	89
TRAVEL BUDGET PLANNER	91
NOTEPAD	92

Isabelle M. Fry

TAHITI

Tahiti
French Polynesia Directions
4.3 ★★★★★ 1,089 reviews
View larger map

Tahiti

Keyboard shortcuts   Map data ©2025 Google   Terms   Report a map error

SCAN THE QR CODE

- Use your device's camera app or go to google and click on lens or a dedicated QR code scanning app.
- Hold your device steady and ensure the QR code fits fully within the frame.
- Let the scanner detect the QR code automatically.
- Click on the link or notification that appears.
- Follow the link or instructions to view the QR code's content.

Tahiti & French Polynesia Travel Guide 2025-2026

FRENCH POLYNESIA

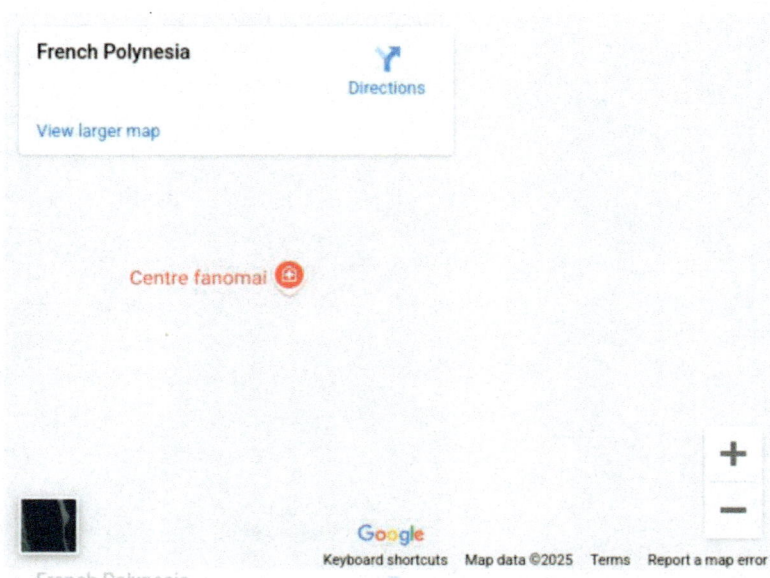

SCAN THE QR CODE

- Use your device's camera app or go to google and click on lens or a dedicated QR code scanning app.
- Hold your device steady and ensure the QR code fits fully within the frame.
- Let the scanner detect the QR code automatically.
- Click on the link or notification that appears.
- Follow the link or instructions to view the QR code's content.

Isabelle M. Fry

INTRODUCTION

Welcome to Tahiti & French Polynesia Travel Guide 2025-2026, your ultimate companion to exploring one of the most enchanting destinations on Earth. This guide is meticulously crafted to provide you with everything you need to know for an unforgettable journey through the paradisiacal islands of Tahiti & French Polynesia. From its breathtaking landscapes and vibrant culture to its rich history and warm hospitality, this region is a dream come true for travelers seeking adventure, relaxation, and a deeper connection with nature.

Tahiti & French Polynesia are comprised of 118 islands and atolls spread across five archipelagos, each offering its own unique charm and allure. Whether you're lounging on the pristine beaches of Bora Bora, diving into the crystal-clear waters of Rangiroa, or hiking through the lush valleys of Moorea, this guide will lead you to the heart of these magical islands.

In this comprehensive travel guide, you'll find detailed information on how to get to Tahiti & French Polynesia, including the best flight options and visa requirements. We'll explore a wide range of accommodation choices, from luxurious overwater bungalows to budget-friendly guesthouses, ensuring that every traveler finds their perfect haven.

Our journey continues with an in-depth look at the must-see attractions, from awe-inspiring natural wonders like lagoons, mountains, and waterfalls to cultural and historical sites that offer a glimpse into the islands' storied past. You'll discover the best spots for adventure and outdoor activities, including snorkeling, diving, hiking, and more.

Savor the flavors of Polynesian cuisine with our guide to local dishes, restaurants, and street food. Learn about the rich cultural heritage of the islands, including traditional dance, music, and art. Stay informed with essential travel tips on currency, banking, safety, and health, ensuring a smooth and worry-free experience.

Whether you're planning a romantic getaway, a family vacation, a solo adventure, or a wellness retreat, Tahiti & French Polynesia Travel Guide 2025-2026 is your trusted resource for making the most of your time in this tropical paradise. Let this guide be your passport to a memorable and enriching experience in one of the world's most beautiful destinations.

CHAPTER 1
WELCOME TO TAHITI & FRENCH POLYNESIA

Imagine a land where the skies are painted in the deepest shades of blue, where emerald-green mountains rise majestically from turquoise lagoons, and the air is filled with the sweet fragrance of tropical flowers. Welcome to Tahiti & French Polynesia—a paradise on Earth.

Tahiti and its surrounding islands are renowned for their stunning natural beauty, vibrant culture, and warm hospitality. This enchanting archipelago, nestled in the heart of the South Pacific, comprises 118 islands and atolls spread across five distinct archipelagos.

WHY VISIT TAHITI & FRENCH POLYNESIA?

Tahiti & French Polynesia is a dream destination that captivates travelers with its irresistible allure. Here are some compelling reasons why this tropical haven should be at the top of your travel list:

- **Breathtaking Landscapes:** From the iconic overwater bungalows of Bora Bora to the lush, verdant valleys of Moorea, the islands boast some of the most picturesque landscapes in the world. Crystal-clear lagoons, pristine beaches, and dramatic volcanic peaks create a postcard-perfect setting.

- **Rich Cultural Heritage:** The islands are steeped in a rich cultural tapestry that blends Polynesian traditions with French influences. Explore ancient marae (sacred sites), attend lively dance performances, and immerse yourself in the warm and welcoming Polynesian way of life.

- **Adventure and Exploration:** Whether you're an adrenaline junkie or a nature enthusiast, there's no shortage of activities to enjoy. Dive into vibrant coral reefs, hike through lush rainforests, paddleboard across serene lagoons, or embark on a thrilling shark and ray encounter.

- **Romantic Getaways:** With its secluded beaches, luxurious resorts, and breathtaking sunsets, Tahiti & French Polynesia is the quintessential destination for couples seeking a romantic escape. Honeymooners and couples will find plenty of intimate spots to create lasting memories.

- **Culinary Delights:** Savor the delectable flavors of Polynesian cuisine, which features an abundance of fresh seafood, tropical fruits, and exotic ingredients. Don't miss out on trying traditional dishes like poisson cru (raw fish salad) and fei (mountain banana).
- **Marine Wonderland:** The marine life around the islands is nothing short of extraordinary. Snorkel or dive in the vibrant coral gardens, swim with manta rays and dolphins, and witness the mesmerizing dance of bioluminescent plankton.

HOW TO USE THIS GUIDE

This travel guide is your ultimate companion to exploring the wonders of Tahiti & French Polynesia. Organized to provide comprehensive and practical information.

- **Plan Your Trip:** Start by reading the sections on getting there, accommodation, and getting around. These chapters will help you arrange your travel logistics, find the best places to stay, and navigate the islands with ease.
- **Explore Must-See Attractions:** Dive into the attractions section to discover the top sights and activities. We've curated a list of must-visit spots, adventurous

experiences, and hidden gems to ensure you don't miss out on anything.

- **Savor Local Flavors:** Use the food and drink chapter to explore the culinary delights of the islands. From fine dining to street food, you'll find recommendations to satisfy your taste buds.
- **Stay Informed:** The laws and guidelines chapter provides essential information on local regulations, safety tips, and health services to ensure a hassle-free and enjoyable stay.
- **Practical Tips and Resources:** The money matters and practical tips chapters offer valuable advice on currency, banking, packing, climate, connectivity, and sustainable travel practices.
- **Day Trips and Excursions:** Discover exciting day trips and neighboring islands worth exploring. Whether you prefer guided tours or DIY adventures, we've got you covered. With this guide in hand, you're all set to embark on an unforgettable journey through Tahiti & French Polynesia. Let's begin your adventure in this paradise!

CHAPTER 2
GETTING THERE
FLIGHTS AND AIRLINES

When planning your journey to Tahiti & French Polynesia, the primary gateway is Faa'a International Airport (PPT) located in Papeete, Tahiti. This modern airport is well-connected to major cities across the globe. Here are some key points to consider:

- **Major Airlines:** Airlines such as Air Tahiti Nui, Air France, Hawaiian Airlines, and Air New Zealand offer direct flights from various international destinations, including Los Angeles, Paris, Auckland, and Tokyo.
- **Connecting Flights**: For those traveling from other parts of the world, connecting flights are available through major hubs like Los Angeles, Auckland, and Tokyo.
- **Domestic Flights:** Once you've arrived in Tahiti, getting around the islands is easy with Air Tahiti, which operates

regular flights to other islands in French Polynesia. These flights offer stunning aerial views of the archipelago.

- **Travel Tips:** Booking flights well in advance can help secure the best deals. Keep an eye out for special promotions and seasonal discounts offered by airlines. Also, consider the baggage policies and any additional fees when booking your tickets.

VISA AND ENTRY REQUIREMENTS

Travelers from many countries, including the United States, Canada, Australia, and most European nations, do not require a visa for stays of up to 90 days in French Polynesia. Here's what you need to know:

- **Passport Validity:** Make sure your passport remains valid for at least six months after your intended departure date.
- **Return Ticket:** Proof of onward or return travel is required upon entry.
- **Health and Safety:** There are no mandatory vaccinations for entry, but it's always a good idea to be up-to-date with routine immunizations. Additionally, considering travel insurance that covers health and medical emergencies is recommended.

- **Customs Regulations:** Be mindful of the customs regulations regarding the importation of goods, especially food and plant products. There are restrictions to protect the local environment from invasive species.

TRANSPORTATION OPTIONS

Upon arrival, there are various transportation options available to help you get around and explore the islands:

- **Ferries and Cruises:** Inter-island ferries and cruises are popular and scenic ways to travel between islands. Companies like Aremiti and Terevau offer regular ferry services between Tahiti, Moorea, and other nearby islands.
- **Domestic Flights:** As mentioned, Air Tahiti provides frequent flights to other islands. This is the fastest way to reach remote locations such as Bora Bora and Rangiroa.
- **Car Rentals:** Renting a car is a convenient option for exploring larger islands like Tahiti and Moorea. Major car rental companies operate at the airport and in major towns. Be sure to familiarize yourself with local driving rules and regulations.
- **Public Transportation:** Public buses, known as "Le Truck," operate on Tahiti and provide a cost-effective

way to travel around the island. Schedules may be limited, so plan accordingly.

- **Taxis and Shuttles:** Taxis are available at the airport and major hotels. Shuttle services can also be arranged through your accommodation for airport transfers and island tours.
- **Biking and Walking:** For a more eco-friendly and leisurely way to explore, consider renting a bicycle or simply walking. Many islands are pedestrian-friendly, and biking is a great way to experience the local scenery up close.

With your travel arrangements sorted, you're all set to embark on an unforgettable journey through the stunning landscapes and vibrant culture of Tahiti & French Polynesia. Up next, we'll delve into where to stay and the various accommodation options available to suit every traveler's needs and preferences.

CHAPTER 3
ACCOMMODATION
LUXURY RESORTS

For those seeking a luxurious escape, Tahiti & French Polynesia are home to some of the world's most opulent resorts. These properties offer unparalleled amenities, breathtaking views, and world-class service. Here are some top picks:

- **The Brando:** Located on the private island of Tetiaroa, The Brando is an eco-friendly resort that offers ultimate luxury and seclusion. Guests can enjoy private villas, gourmet dining, and activities such as snorkeling, paddleboarding, and cultural tours.
- **Four Seasons Resort Bora Bora:** This iconic resort features overwater bungalows with stunning views of Mount Otemanu. Guests can indulge in spa treatments, fine dining, and a range of water sports.

- **St. Regis Bora Bora Resort:** Known for its elegant overwater villas and lagoonarium, the St. Regis offer a unique blend of luxury and adventure. Activities include jet skiing, deep-sea fishing, and sunset cruises.

BOUTIQUE HOTELS

For a more intimate and personalized experience, boutique hotels provide a charming alternative to large resorts. These properties often emphasize local culture and unique design:

- **Moorea Pearl Resort & Spa:** Located on the island of Moorea, this boutique hotel offers garden bungalows, beachfront rooms, and overwater bungalows. The resort features a spa, infinity pool, and easy access to nearby attractions.
- **Le Taha'a Island Resort & Spa:** Nestled on a private islet, this resort offers luxurious suites and villas surrounded by turquoise waters. Guests can enjoy

gourmet dining, spa treatments, and activities like snorkeling and kayaking.
- **Hotel Kia Ora Resort & Spa:** Situated on the island of Rangiroa, this boutique hotel features beachfront and garden bungalows, as well as overwater suites. The resort offers a range of activities, including diving, fishing, and cultural excursions.

BUDGET-FRIENDLY STAYS

Travelers on a budget need not miss out on the beauty and charm of Tahiti & French Polynesia. There are plenty of affordable accommodation options that provide comfort and convenience without breaking the bank:

- **Pension Havaiki Lodge**: Located on the island of Fakarava, this family-run guesthouse offers beachfront bungalows and a welcoming atmosphere. Guests can enjoy activities such as snorkeling, kayaking, and exploring the island's natural beauty.

- **Fare Suisse:** This budget-friendly guesthouse in Papeete offers clean and comfortable rooms, a friendly atmosphere, and easy access to local attractions. It's an excellent base for exploring Tahiti.
- **Taaroa Lodge:** Located on the island of Tahiti, Taaroa Lodge offers affordable rooms and bungalows in a tranquil setting. Guests can enjoy the on-site swimming pool, garden, and proximity to the beach.

OVERWATER BUNGALOWS: THE ULTIMATE EXPERIENCE

No trip to Tahiti & French Polynesia is complete without experiencing an overwater bungalow. These iconic accommodations offer direct access to the lagoon, stunning views, and a sense of serenity:

- Conrad Bora Bora Nui: This luxury resort offers spacious overwater villas with private plunge pools, outdoor showers, and glass-bottom floors. Guests can enjoy fine dining, a spa, and a range of water activities.
- **InterContinental Bora Bora Resort & Thalasso Spa:** Known for its overwater bungalows with direct lagoon access, this resort offers a unique experience with its thalasso therapy spa, gourmet restaurants, and water sports.
- **Sofitel Moorea Ia Ora Beach Resort:** Located on the island of Moorea, this resort features overwater bungalows with stunning views of the lagoon and Mount Rotui. Guests can enjoy water sports, a spa, and fine dining.
- **Alternative Accommodation:** Airbnb, Guesthouses, and Camping. For a more authentic and local experience, consider staying in alternative accommodations such as Airbnbs, guesthouses, or even camping:Airbnb: There are plenty of Airbnb options available across the islands, ranging from cozy apartments to entire villas. This option allows travelers to experience local living and often provides more flexibility and affordability.
- **Guesthouses:** Family-run guesthouses and pensions offer a warm and welcoming atmosphere. These

accommodations often include meals and provide an opportunity to connect with local hosts and learn about their culture.

- Camping: For the adventurous traveler, camping is an option on some of the islands. There are designated campgrounds and eco-friendly lodges that offer a unique way to experience the natural beauty of Tahiti & French Polynesia.

No matter your preference or budget, Tahiti & French Polynesia have a wide range of accommodation options to suit every traveler. Up next, we'll explore the best ways to get around and navigate the islands, ensuring you can make the most of your time in this tropical paradise.

CHAPTER 4
GETTING AROUND
PUBLIC TRANSPORTATION

Public transportation on the islands varies, and understanding your options can help you navigate efficiently:

- **Le Truck:** On Tahiti and some of the other larger islands, "Le Truck" offers a cost-effective way to get around. These colorful, open-air buses are a charming way to travel and connect with locals. However, schedules can be unpredictable, so it's best to check ahead or ask locals for the latest information.
- **Buses:** Regular buses operate on some islands, providing a more structured service. Papeete, the capital city of Tahiti, has a reliable bus network that connects major parts of the city and surrounding areas.

Car Rentals

Renting a car is a convenient option, especially if you plan to explore larger islands at your own pace:

- **Rental Agencies:** Major car rental companies, including Avis, Hertz, and Europcar, have offices at the airport and in major towns. It is highly recommended to book in advance, especially during peak travel times.

- **Driving Tips:** Driving is on the right side of the road. Speed limits are generally low, and road conditions are usually good, but be cautious on narrow or winding roads. Obtaining an international driving permit is strongly advised.

Biking And Walking

For a more leisurely and eco-friendly way to explore, consider biking or walking:

- **Bike Rentals:** Many hotels and guesthouses offer bike rentals. Biking is an excellent way to explore smaller islands and coastal areas at your own pace.
- **Walking Tours:** Walking tours are a fantastic way to immerse yourself in the local culture and scenery. Guided tours are available, or you can explore independently with a good map or GPS.

Water Taxis And Boat Services

Given the island nature of Tahiti & French Polynesia, water transport is essential:

- **Water Taxis:** Water taxis are available for short trips between islands or to reach specific attractions. These can be arranged through hotels or local operators.

- **Boat Services:** Regular boat services operate between islands. For example, the Aremiti and Terevau ferries run frequent services between Tahiti and Moorea. Private boat charters are also available for more personalized experiences.

Domestic Flights

For longer distances and to reach remote islands, domestic flights are the most efficient option:

- **Air Tahiti:** The main domestic airline, Air Tahiti, operates flights to many islands in the archipelago. Flights offer stunning aerial views and are relatively short, making them a convenient choice for island hopping.
- **Booking Tips:** Book flights in advance to secure the best fares and availability. Be mindful of baggage restrictions, especially if traveling with sports equipment or large items.
- **Air Moorea:** This airline provides frequent flights between Tahiti and Moorea, with a short flight time of just 15 minutes.
- **Booking Tips:** Early booking is recommended as flights can fill up quickly, especially during peak tourist seasons. Check for any promotional fares that may be available.

- **Air Archipels**: Serving various islands in the Tuamotu and Gambier archipelagos, Air Archipels offers flights to destinations such as Rangiroa, Manihi, and Rikitea.
- **Booking Tips:** It's important to confirm flight schedules and availability as services to these remote islands may be less frequent. Consider booking a flexible ticket in case of any schedule changes.
- **Tahiti Helicopters:** For a unique and thrilling experience, Tahiti Helicopters offers helicopter transfers and scenic flights between islands, providing breathtaking aerial views.
- **Booking** Tips: Advance reservations are essential, especially for scenic flights. Be sure to check the weight limitations and baggage policies for helicopter travel.

With these transportation options, you'll have the flexibility and convenience to explore the diverse landscapes and vibrant culture of Tahiti & French Polynesia. Next, we'll delve into the must-see attractions that await you on these enchanting islands.

CHAPTER 5
MUST-SEE ATTRACTIONS
NATURAL WONDERS: LAGOONS, MOUNTAINS, AND WATERFALLS

Tahiti & French Polynesia boast some of the world's most breathtaking natural wonders. Here are a few highlights:

- **Bora Bora Lagoon:** Often referred to as the "Pearl of the Pacific," Bora Bora's lagoon is a stunning turquoise paradise. The calm, clear waters are perfect for snorkeling, diving, and other water activities. Don't miss the opportunity to take a lagoon tour and experience the vibrant marine life up close.
- **Mount Otemanu:** Rising majestically from the island of Bora Bora, Mount Otemanu is an extinct volcano offering

incredible hiking opportunities. The summit provides panoramic views of the island and surrounding lagoon. It's a must-visit for adventure seekers and nature lovers

- **Fautaua Waterfall:** Located on the island of Tahiti, Fautaua Waterfall is one of the tallest waterfalls in the world. The hike to the waterfall is challenging but rewarding, with lush jungle scenery and the refreshing mist of the falls greeting you at the end.

- **The Blue Lagoon of Rangiroa:** Known for its otherworldly beauty, the Blue Lagoon in Rangiroa is a secluded paradise. The vibrant blue waters are surrounded by white sand and coral reefs, creating a perfect spot for swimming, snorkeling, and relaxation.

BEACHES: BEST SPOTS FOR SUN, SAND, AND SURF

The islands of Tahiti & French Polynesia are home to some of the most beautiful beaches in the world. Here are a few that should be on your list:

- **Matira Beach:** Located on the island of Bora Bora, Matira Beach is often regarded as one of the best beaches in the world. Its powdery white sand, crystal-clear waters, and gentle waves make it an ideal spot for swimming, sunbathing, and beachcombing.

- **Temae Beach:** Situated on the island of Moorea, Temae Beach offers stunning views of the lagoon and distant Tahiti. The beach is perfect for snorkeling, with abundant marine life just a few meters from the shore. It's also a great spot for picnicking and enjoying the sunset.
- **Tikehau Beach:** Known for its pink sand, Tikehau Beach is a unique and beautiful destination. The calm, shallow waters make it an excellent spot for swimming and snorkeling. The island's relaxed atmosphere is perfect for unwinding and enjoying the natural beauty.
- **Papara Beach:** For those looking to catch some waves, Papara Beach on Tahiti is a popular surf spot. The black sand beach is known for its consistent surf breaks, attracting surfers from around the world. Even if you're not a surfer, the beach is a great place to relax and watch the action.

HISTORICAL SITES AND MUSEUMS

Tahiti & French Polynesia have a rich cultural history, and there are several historical sites and museums to explore:

- **Paul Gauguin Museum:** Situated on Tahiti, the Paul Gauguin Museum is dedicated to the famous French painter who spent the last years of his life in French Polynesia. The museum houses a collection of his works, as well as exhibits on his life and influence. It's a must-visit for art enthusiasts.
- **James Norman Hall Museum:** This museum, located in Arue on Tahiti, is dedicated to the American author James Norman Hall. The museum is housed in his former residence and showcases his life, works, and contributions to literature. It's a charming and informative stop for literature lovers.
- **Taputapuatea Marae:** Located on the island of Raiatea, Taputapuatea Marae is a UNESCO World Heritage Site and one of the most important cultural sites in Polynesia. The marae complex was a central hub for Polynesian navigation and religious ceremonies. Visitors can explore the site and learn about its historical and cultural significance.

Adventure And Outdoor Activities

For those seeking adventure and outdoor experiences, Tahiti & French Polynesia offer a plethora of options:

- **Diving and Snorkeling:** The islands are renowned for their vibrant coral reefs and abundant marine life. Popular dive sites include the Tiputa Pass in Rangiroa, the Blue Hole in Fakarava, and the Coral Gardens in Bora Bora. Snorkeling is equally rewarding, with opportunities to see colorful fish, rays, and even sharks.
- **Hiking:** From the lush valleys of Moorea to the volcanic peaks of Tahiti, there are numerous hiking trails to explore. Popular hikes include the Mount Rotui hike on Moorea, the Aorai Mountain hike on Tahiti, and the Three Coconuts Pass hike on Tahiti.
- **Lagoon Tours:** Take a guided lagoon tour to explore the stunning waters of Bora Bora, Moorea, or Taha'a. These tours often include stops for snorkeling, swimming with rays and sharks, and enjoying a traditional Polynesian picnic on a motu (small islet).
- **Water Sports:** Whether you're into kayaking, paddleboarding, jet skiing, or sailing, the calm waters of the lagoons provide the perfect playground for water sports enthusiasts. Rentals and guided tours are readily available.

Unique Experiences

Tahiti & French Polynesia offer several unique experiences that you won't find anywhere else:

- **Swimming with Sharks and Stingrays**: In the lagoons of Bora Bora and Moorea, you can safely swim with blacktip reef sharks and stingrays. Guided tours provide a thrilling and unforgettable experience, allowing you to get up close to these fascinating creatures.
- **Lagoonarium:** The Lagoonarium in Bora Bora is a natural aquarium where you can swim with a variety of marine life in a safe environment. It's an excellent option for families and those looking for a more controlled snorkeling experience.
- **Pearl Farms:** Visit a pearl farm on one of the islands, such as Taha'a or Rangiroa, to learn about the cultivation of Tahitian black pearls. Many farms offer tours that include demonstrations of the pearl farming process and the opportunity to purchase pearls directly from the source. With so many incredible attractions and activities to choose from, you're sure to have an unforgettable adventure in Tahiti & French Polynesia.

CHAPTER 6
FOOD AND DRINK
Traditional Tahitian Cuisine

Tahitian cuisine is a delightful blend of Polynesian flavors, French influences, and the freshest local ingredients. The islands' culinary traditions are deeply rooted in the natural bounty of the land and sea. Here are some traditional dishes that you must try:

- **Poisson Cru:** Often considered the national dish of Tahiti, poisson cru is a delicious raw fish salad. Fresh fish, usually tuna, is marinated in lime juice and mixed with coconut milk, tomatoes, onions, and cucumbers. The result is a refreshing and flavorful dish that is a must-try for any visitor.
- **Ma'a Tahiti:** This traditional feast consists of a variety of dishes cooked in an underground oven called an ahima'a. Dishes may include taro, breadfruit, pork,

chicken, and fish, all wrapped in banana leaves and slow-cooked to perfection. The communal meal is often enjoyed during special occasions and festivals.

- **Firi Firi:** These delightful coconut-flavored doughnuts are a popular breakfast treat. Firi firi are deep-fried to a golden brown and often served with a cup of hot coffee or tea. They are the perfect way to start your day in Tahiti.
- **Poe:** Poe is a traditional Polynesian dessert made from ripe fruits such as bananas, papayas, or mangoes. The fruit is mixed with starch, usually arrowroot or cornstarch, and baked until it becomes a thick pudding. It is typically served with a generous drizzle of coconut milk.

MUST-TRY DISHES

In addition to traditional dishes, there are several other culinary delights that you should sample during your visit:

- **Chevrettes:** These freshwater shrimp are often served grilled or sautéed with garlic and herbs. They are a delicious and popular appetizer.
- **Po'e Tahiti:** This is a local variation of the traditional Polynesian dessert, po'e. It is made with a base of taro or banana and often flavored with vanilla or coconut milk.
- **Tahitian Vanilla:** Tahiti is famous for its vanilla, which is often used in both sweet and savory dishes. Be sure to try vanilla-infused dishes and desserts, such as vanilla-flavored sauces, cakes, and ice creams.
- **Uru (Breadfruit):** Breadfruit is a staple in Tahitian cuisine and can be prepared in various ways, including roasted, fried, or mashed. It is often served as a side dish or used in stews and curries.

BEST RESTAURANTS AND LOCAL EATERIES

Tahiti & French Polynesia offer a diverse range of dining options, from fine dining restaurants to casual local eateries. Here are some top recommendations:

- **La Villa Mahana (Bora Bora)**: This intimate, high-end restaurant offers a gourmet dining experience with a focus on French and Polynesian fusion cuisine. Reservations are essential due to its limited seating and popularity.

- **Le Coco's (Tahiti):** Located in Punaauia, Le Coco's offers stunning views of the lagoon and Moorea. The menu features a mix of French and local dishes, with an emphasis on fresh seafood and seasonal ingredients.

- **Snack Mahana (Moorea):** For a more casual dining experience, Snack Mahana is a popular beachfront eatery serving delicious local dishes. The poisson cru and grilled fish are highly recommended.

- **Bloody Mary's (Bora Bora):** This iconic restaurant is known for its laid-back atmosphere and fresh seafood. Diners can choose their meal from a display of fresh catches, and the chefs will prepare it to order.

- **Le Lotus (Tahiti):** Located at the InterContinental Tahiti Resort & Spa, Le Lotus offers fine dining with a stunning overwater setting. The restaurant specializes in French cuisine with a Polynesian twist.

Street Food And Market Delights

Exploring local markets and street food stalls is a great way to experience the authentic flavors of Tahiti & French Polynesia:

- **Papeete Market (Tahiti):** This bustling market is the perfect place to sample local street food and shop for fresh produce, seafood, and handicrafts. Be sure to try the variety of snacks and treats available, including firi firi and coconut bread.
- **Fare Miti (Moorea):** This charming market offers a range of street food options, from grilled fish to tropical fruit salads. It's a great spot to enjoy a quick and tasty meal while soaking up the local atmosphere.
- **Food Trucks:** Known locally as "roulottes," food trucks are a popular dining option in many towns and villages. They offer a variety of dishes, including crepes, grilled meats, and seafood, all at affordable prices. The waterfront area in Papeete is particularly known for its vibrant roulotte scene.

Drinks And Nightlife

From tropical cocktails to traditional Polynesian brews, Tahiti & French Polynesia offer a vibrant drinks and nightlife scen

- **Hinano Beer:** This locally brewed beer is a favorite among both locals and visitors. It's light and refreshing, perfect for enjoying on a sunny beach day.
- **Mai Tai:** A classic tropical cocktail, the Mai Tai is a must-try. Made with rum, lime juice, orgeat syrup, and orange liqueur, it's a delicious and refreshing drink to enjoy at sunset.
- **Local Rum:** Tahiti produces its own rum, which is often flavored with vanilla or tropical fruits. Be sure to try a rum cocktail or sample the rum straight.
- **Nightclubs and Bars:** The islands have a variety of nightlife options, from laid-back beach bars to lively nightclubs. Popular spots include the Morrison's Café in Papeete, which offers live music and a vibrant atmosphere, and the Bora Bora Yacht Club, known for its beautiful waterfront setting and relaxed vibe.

With its diverse and delectable culinary scene, Tahiti & French Polynesia offer a feast for the senses. Up next, we'll delve into the rich culture and customs of the islands, providing insights into the local way of life and how to connect with the warm and welcoming Polynesian people.

CHAPTER 7
CULTURE AND CUSTOMS
Understanding Polynesian Culture

Tahiti & French Polynesia are steeped in rich cultural heritage that beautifully blends ancient Polynesian traditions with French influences. The islands' vibrant culture is evident in their art, music, dance, and daily life. Here are a few key elements to help you appreciate and understand this unique culture:

- **Polynesian Dance (Ori Tahiti):** One of the most captivating aspects of Polynesian culture is the traditional dance known as Ori Tahiti. Such interactive experiences are both engaging and educational. The dancers, adorned in elaborate costumes made from natural materials, use graceful movements to tell stories and express emotions. Attending a dance performance is a must-do for any visitor.

- **Tattooing (Tatau):** Tattoos hold deep cultural significance in Polynesian society. They are not just body art but also symbols of identity, status, and heritage. The traditional tattooing process is intricate and often painful, involving the use of hand-tapped tools. Today, many locals proudly display their tattoos, which are rich in symbolism and meaning.

- **Music and Instruments:** Polynesian music is an integral part of the islands' cultural fabric. The sounds of ukuleles, drums, and conch shells are often heard during traditional ceremonies and celebrations. Music and dance are closely linked, and the rhythmic beats create an enchanting atmosphere that immerses visitors in the local culture.
- **Art and Craftsmanship:** The islands are home to talented artisans who create beautiful works of art using traditional techniques. From intricate wood carvings to stunning tapa cloth (bark cloth) creations, these crafts reflect the rich cultural heritage of Polynesia. Visitors can explore local markets and workshops to purchase unique souvenirs and learn about the craftsmanship behind these art forms.

Local Festivals And Events

Throughout the year, Tahiti & French Polynesia host various festivals and events that celebrate their culture, history, and natural beauty. Here are some noteworthy events to consider attending:

- **Heiva i Tahiti:** This month-long festival, held annually in July, is one of the most important cultural events in French Polynesia. It features traditional dance competitions, music performances, sports events, and craft exhibitions. Heiva i Tahiti is a vibrant celebration of Polynesian heritage and offers visitors a deep insight into local traditions.

- **Tattoo Festival:** The annual Tattoo Festival celebrates the art of tattooing and its cultural significance in Polynesia. The event brings together tattoo artists from around the world, showcasing their skills and offering live demonstrations. It's a fascinating event for those interested in the history and meaning behind Polynesian tattoos.
- **Bastille Day:** Celebrated on July 14th, Bastille Day is a national holiday that commemorates the French Revolution. In French Polynesia, the day is marked with parades, fireworks, and various festivities. It's a great opportunity to experience the unique blend of French and Polynesian cultures.
- **Billabong Pro Tahiti:** For surf enthusiasts, the Billabong Pro Tahiti is an exciting event to watch. This professional surfing competition is held annually in Teahupo'o, known for its powerful and challenging waves. The event attracts top surfers from around the world and offers thrilling action for spectators.

Art And Craftsmanship

Exploring the art and craftsmanship of Tahiti & French Polynesia provides a deeper appreciation for the islands' cultural heritage:

- **Tapa Cloth:** Tapa cloth is a traditional fabric made from the bark of mulberry trees. The process of creating tapa involves soaking, beating, and decorating the bark to produce intricate designs. Tapa cloth is used in various ceremonial and everyday items, such as clothing, mats, and wall hangings.

- **Wood Carving:** Polynesian wood carvings are renowned for their intricate details and cultural symbolism. Commonly carved items include tikis (wooden statues), bowls, and tools. These carvings often depict gods, ancestors, and elements of nature, reflecting the deep spiritual connection of the Polynesian people.

- **Pearl Jewelry:** Tahiti is famous for its black pearls, which are cultivated in the pristine waters of the islands. Local artisans create stunning jewelry pieces, including necklaces, earrings, and bracelets, using these lustrous pearls. Visiting a pearl farm or jewelry shop is a wonderful way to learn about the cultivation process and find a unique souvenir.

Etiquette And Respectful Behavior

Understanding and respecting local customs and etiquette is essential when visiting Tahiti & French Polynesia. Here are some guidelines to ensure you have a respectful and enjoyable experience:

- **Greetings:** A warm greeting goes a long way. The traditional Polynesian greeting involves a light kiss on each cheek, known as "la bise." However, a friendly handshake is also acceptable. To greet someone in Tahitian, you can say "Ia Orana" (hello) or "Mauruuru" (thank you).
- **Dress Code:** While the islands have a relaxed and casual atmosphere, it's important to dress modestly when visiting villages, cultural sites, and religious places. Swimwear is appropriate for the beach, but cover-ups are recommended when walking around public areas.
- **Gifts and Offerings:** When invited to a local's home or event, it's customary to bring a small gift, such as fruits, flowers, or a token from your home country. This gesture is appreciated and shows respect for the hosts.
- **Respect for Nature:** The natural environment is sacred to the Polynesian people. Be mindful of your impact on the environment by following responsible travel

practices, such as not littering, avoiding damaging coral reefs, and respecting wildlife.

LANGUAGE AND COMMUNICATION

While French is the official language of Tahiti & French Polynesia, many locals also speak Tahitian and English. Here are some tips for effective communication:

Basic Tahitian Phrases:

- Hello: Ia Orana (yo-rah-nah)
- Thank You: Mauruuru (mah-roo-roo)
- Please: 'Oa'o'a (oh-ah-oh-ah)
- Yes: E (eh)
- No: Aita (eye-tah)

Language Etiquette: While many locals speak English, making an effort to use basic Tahitian or French phrases is appreciated. It shows respect for the local culture and can enhance your interactions with the community.

- Communication Tools: Having a translation app or phrasebook on hand can be helpful when navigating the islands. Additionally, many hotels, restaurants, and tour operators have staff who speak multiple languages, making communication easier for international visitors.

CHAPTER 8
LAWS AND GUIDELINES
IMPORTANT LAWS FOR VISITORS

To ensure a safe and enjoyable stay in Tahiti & French Polynesia, it's essential to be aware of the local laws and regulations. Here are some important things to keep in mind:

- **Respect for Local Customs:** The Polynesian culture is deeply rooted in traditions and customs. It is important to show respect for these customs, especially when visiting sacred sites, participating in cultural activities, or interacting with local communities. Dress modestly and always ask for permission before taking photographs of people or private property.

- **Alcohol Consumption:** The legal drinking age in French Polynesia is 18 years old. Alcohol is widely available, but it is important to consume it responsibly. Public intoxication is frowned upon, and it is illegal to drink alcohol in public places, such as streets and parks.

- **Drug Laws:** French Polynesia has strict laws regarding drug possession and use. The possession, use, or trafficking of illegal drugs is a serious offense and can result in severe penalties, including imprisonment. It is important to avoid any involvement with illegal substances during your stay.

- **Environmental Protection:** The islands' natural beauty is one of their greatest assets, and there are strict laws in place to protect the environment. Avoid damaging coral reefs, littering, or disturbing wildlife. Some areas, such as marine reserves and national parks, have specific regulations to preserve their ecosystems. Respect these rules to help maintain the pristine condition of the islands.

- **Safety Regulations:** Water safety is a priority in French Polynesia, especially for activities such as swimming, snorkeling, and diving. Always follow safety guidelines provided by tour operators and adhere to warning signs on beaches. Use sunscreen and stay hydrated to protect yourself from the tropical sun.

- **Driving Laws:** If you plan to rent a car, familiarize yourself with local driving laws. Driving is on the right side of the road, and seat belts are mandatory for all passengers. Speed limits are enforced, and driving under the influence of alcohol is strictly prohibited. Always carry your driver's license and rental agreement when driving.

SAFETY TIPS AND PRECAUTIONS

While Tahiti & French Polynesia are generally safe destinations, it is important to take common-sense precautions to ensure your well-being:

- **Stay Informed:** Stay updated on any travel advisories or safety warnings issued by your government or local authorities. Follow their recommendations to avoid any potential risks.
- **Protect Your Belongings:** Petty theft can occur in tourist areas, so keep an eye on your belongings and avoid displaying valuable items. Use hotel safes to store passports, money, and other important documents.
- **Health and Hygiene:** The tropical climate can pose health challenges, such as dehydration, sunburn, and insect bites. Drink plenty of water, use sunscreen, and apply insect repellent to protect yourself. If you plan to participate in outdoor activities, wear appropriate clothing and footwear.
- **Medical Services:** French Polynesia has a good healthcare system, with hospitals and medical clinics available on the main islands. It is advisable to have travel insurance that covers medical expenses and emergency evacuation. Know the location of nearby medical facilities and carry any essential medications with you.

- **Natural Disasters:** While rare, natural disasters such as cyclones and earthquakes can occur. Stay informed about weather conditions and follow any instructions or evacuation orders issued by local authorities. Familiarize yourself with emergency procedures and have a basic plan in place.

Health And Medical Services

Access to healthcare is an important consideration when traveling. Here are some key points about health and medical services in Tahiti & French Polynesia:

- **Healthcare Facilities:** The main islands, such as Tahiti, Moorea, and Bora Bora, have hospitals and medical clinics that provide a range of services. Papeete, the capital city of Tahiti, has the largest hospital, Centre Hospitalier de Polynésie Française, which offers comprehensive medical care.
- **Travel Insurance:** It is highly recommended to have travel insurance that covers medical expenses, emergency evacuation, and trip cancellations. Check with your insurance provider to ensure you have adequate coverage for your stay.
- **Pharmacies:** Pharmacies are available in major towns and tourist areas. They provide a range of over-the-

counter medications, prescription drugs, and medical supplies. If you have specific medical needs, it is advisable to bring an adequate supply of your medications.

- **Vaccinations:** While there are no mandatory vaccinations for entry into French Polynesia, it is recommended to be up-to-date with routine vaccinations, such as measles, mumps, rubella, and tetanus. Consult with your healthcare provider for any additional vaccinations that may be recommended based on your travel plans.
- **Emergency Services:** In case of a medical emergency, dial 15 for an ambulance or 17 for the police. It is also a good idea to have the contact information of your embassy or consulate in case you need assistance.
- Telemedicine Services: Some remote islands may have limited access to medical facilities. Telemedicine services are available and can connect you with healthcare professionals via video call for consultations, prescriptions, and medical advice.
- Health and Wellness Retreats: For travelers seeking wellness, several resorts in French Polynesia offer health and wellness retreats. These retreats include specialized

programs such as detox, yoga, meditation, and spa treatments, promoting overall well-being.

- Preventive Measures: Take preventive measures to avoid illnesses common in tropical climates, such as using insect repellent to prevent mosquito-borne diseases, staying hydrated, and practicing good hygiene.

By familiarizing yourself with the local laws, safety guidelines, and healthcare services, you can ensure a smooth and worry-free stay in Tahiti & French Polynesia. Up next, we'll explore practical tips on money matters, including currency, banking, and tipping etiquette, to help you manage your finances during your trip.

CHAPTER 9
MONEY MATTERS
Currency And Exchange Rates

The official currency of Tahiti & French Polynesia is the French Pacific Franc (XPF), also known as the CFP Franc. Here's what you should know about managing money during your trip:

- **Currency Exchange:** The XPF is pegged to the Euro, with a fixed exchange rate of 1 Euro = 119.33 XPF. Currency exchange services are available at the airport, banks, and major hotels. It's a good idea to exchange some money upon arrival for immediate expenses.

- **ATMs:** ATMs are widely available on the main islands, such as Tahiti, Moorea, and Bora Bora. They accept major international debit and credit cards, including Visa and MasterCard. Inform your bank of your travel plans to avoid any potential issues with using your cards abroad.

- **Credit and Debit Cards:** Credit and debit cards are accepted at most hotels, restaurants, and shops. However, it's advisable to carry some cash for small purchases, markets, and remote areas where card payment may not be possible.

- **Tipping Etiquette:** Tipping is not a common practice in Tahiti & French Polynesia, as service charges are usually included in the bill. However, if you receive exceptional service, leaving a small tip as a gesture of appreciation is welcomed.

Banking And Atms

Banking services in Tahiti & French Polynesia are reliable and convenient. Here's what you need to know:

- **Banks:** Major banks, such as Banque de Tahiti, Banque Socredo, and Banque de Polynésie, have branches on the main islands. They offer a range of services, including currency exchange, traveler's checks, and international transfers.

- **ATM Locations:** ATMs are located at the airport, in major towns, and at popular tourist spots. Most ATMs provide instructions in multiple languages and dispense XPF. Keep in mind that some remote islands may have limited or no ATM facilities, so plan accordingly.

- **Banking Hours:** Banks are generally open from 8:00 AM to 4:00 PM, Monday to Friday. Some branches may have shorter hours on Saturdays. It's advisable to complete any banking transactions during these hours.

Tipping Etiquette

While tipping is not customary in Tahiti & French Polynesia, here are some guidelines to help you navigate tipping practices:

- **Restaurants:** Service charges are typically included in the bill, so tipping is not expected. However, if you receive exceptional service, you can leave a small tip (around 5-10%) to show your appreciation.
- **Hotels:** Tipping hotel staff, such as porters and housekeepers, is not common practice. If you wish to tip for exceptional service, a small amount (around 200-500 XPF) is appreciated.
- **Tour Guides:** If you participate in guided tours and excursions, it's customary to tip the guide if you are satisfied with the experience. A tip of 1,000-2,000 XPF is considered generous and appreciated.
- **Taxis:** Tipping taxi drivers is not expected, but rounding up the fare to the nearest convenient amount as a gesture of appreciation is a common practice.

PRACTICAL TIPS FOR MANAGING MONEY

To ensure a smooth and hassle-free experience with money matters during your trip, consider these practical tips:

- **Notify Your Bank:** Let your bank know about your travel itinerary to prevent your card from being flagged for unusual activity Keep in mind that there are two distinct seasons to consider when planning your trip.

- **Carry Multiple Payment Methods:** It's advisable to carry a mix of cash, credit cards, and debit cards to ensure you have payment options in case of emergencies or technical issues.
- **Check Exchange Rates:** Keep an eye on exchange rates and consider exchanging money when rates are favorable. Avoid exchanging large sums at airports, as rates may be less favorable compared to banks and authorized exchange bureaus.
- **Secure Your Valuables:** Use hotel safes to store cash, cards, and important documents. Avoid carrying large amounts of cash and be mindful of your belongings, especially in crowded areas.

By being well-prepared and informed about money matters, you can manage your finances with ease and enjoy a worry-free stay in Tahiti & French Polynesia. Up next, we'll explore practical tips on packing, climate, connectivity, and sustainable travel practices to help you make the most of your trip.

CHAPTER 10
PRACTICAL TIPS
PACKING LIST AND TRAVEL ESSENTIALS

Preparing for your trip to Tahiti & French Polynesia requires thoughtful packing to ensure you have everything you need for a comfortable and enjoyable stay. Here's a comprehensive packing list to guide you:

Clothing:

- Lightweight, breathable clothing (cotton, linen, or moisture-wicking fabrics)
- Swimwear and cover-ups
- Casual outfits for day trips and excursions
- Dressy attire for dining out and special occasions
- Light jacket or sweater for cooler evenings
- Rain poncho or waterproof jacket

Footwear:

- Comfortable walking shoes or sandals
- Flip-flops for the beach
- Water shoes for snorkeling and water activities
- Hiking boots or sturdy shoes for outdoor adventures

Accessories:

- Wide-brimmed hat or cap
- Sunglasses with UV protection
- Beach bag or tote
- Lightweight backpack or daypack
- Reusable water bottle

Health and Hygiene:

- Sunscreen with high SPF (reef-safe recommended)
- Insect repellent
- Personal hygiene items (toothbrush, toothpaste, deodorant, etc.)
- Medications and a basic first aid kit
- Hand sanitizer and wet wipes

Technology and Gadgets:

- Smartphone and charger
- Camera or GoPro for capturing memories
- Portable power bank
- Travel adapter and voltage converter

Travel Documents:

- Passport (with at least six months' validity)
- Travel insurance details

- Copies of important documents (passport, tickets, accommodation reservations)
- Credit cards and some cash in local currency

CLIMATE AND WEATHER: BEST TIME TO VISIT

Tahiti & French Polynesia enjoy a tropical climate, characterized by warm temperatures and abundant sunshine year-round. Here are some suggestions for being a considerate and responsible traveler:

- **Dry Season (May to October):** This is the most popular time to visit, with pleasant temperatures ranging from 24°C to 28°C (75°F to 82°F). The weather is generally dry and sunny, making it ideal for outdoor activities, beach relaxation, and water sports. This is also the peak tourist season, so advance bookings are recommended.
- **Wet Season (November to April):** During this period, temperatures range from 25°C to 30°C (77°F to 86°F), and the weather is more humid with occasional rain showers and thunderstorms. While the rain can be heavy, it usually clears quickly, leaving plenty of time for outdoor activities. The wet season is also the best time for diving, as the marine life is more active. Travel during this season can be more affordable, with fewer crowds.

CONNECTIVITY: INTERNET AND PHONE SERVICES

Staying connected during your trip is important for communication and navigation. Here's what you need to know about internet and phone services in Tahiti & French Polynesia:

- **Internet Access:** Most hotels, resorts, and guesthouses offer Wi-Fi, but the quality and speed can vary. In major towns and tourist areas, you'll find internet cafes and public Wi-Fi hotspots. Consider purchasing a local SIM card with a data plan for more reliable internet access.

- **Phone Services:** Major mobile carriers, such as Vini and Vodafone, provide good coverage on the main islands. You can purchase a prepaid SIM card at the airport or in major towns. Ensure your phone is unlocked before traveling to use a local SIM card. International roaming is also available but can be expensive.

- **Communication Apps:** Using communication apps like WhatsApp, Skype, or FaceTime can help you stay in touch with family and friends without incurring high phone charges. These apps work well with Wi-Fi or mobile data.

Sustainable Travel: How To Be A Responsible Tourist

Tahiti & French Polynesia are known for their pristine natural beauty, and it's important to practice sustainable travel to preserve the environment and support local communities. Support local artisans by purchasing souvenirs and products made by them:

- **Reduce Plastic Waste:** Bring reusable water bottles, shopping bags, and containers to minimize single-use plastic. Many hotels and resorts provide filtered water stations.
- **Respect Wildlife:** Observe marine life and wildlife from a distance and avoid touching or disturbing them. Participate in responsible wildlife tours that prioritize animal welfare.
- **Support Local Businesses:** Choose locally-owned accommodations, restaurants, and tour operators to support the local economy. Conserve Resources: Practice mindful usage of water and energy.

Buying local products helps support the community and maintain traditional craftsmanship. Take shorter showers, turn off lights and air conditioning when not in use, and opt for eco-friendly accommodations.

Follow Leave No Trace Principles: Dispose of waste properly, stick to designated trails, and leave natural areas as you found them. Avoid taking shells, coral, or plants as souvenirs.

By following these practical tips, you can ensure a smooth and enjoyable trip while minimizing your environmental impact and contributing to the well-being of the local community. Up next, we'll explore exciting day trips and excursions to neighboring islands, offering unique experiences and adventures beyond the main destinations.

CHAPTER 11
DAY TRIPS AND EXCURSIONS
NEIGHBORING ISLANDS: MUST-VISIT DESTINATIONS

Exploring the neighboring islands of Tahiti & French Polynesia offers unique experiences and adventures beyond the main destinations. Here are some must-visit islands for memorable day trips and excursions:

- **Moorea:** Just a short ferry ride from Tahiti, Moorea is a popular day trip destination. Known for its stunning landscapes, crystal-clear lagoons, and lush mountains, Moorea offers a range of activities, including snorkeling, hiking, and exploring pineapple plantations. Don't miss the Belvedere Lookout for panoramic views of the island.

- **Taha'a:** Often referred to as the "Vanilla Island," Taha'a is known for its fragrant vanilla plantations and serene atmosphere. Take a guided tour of a vanilla farm, visit the coral gardens for snorkeling, and enjoy a traditional Polynesian picnic on a secluded motu (islet).

- **Raiatea:** As the cultural and historical heart of French Polynesia, Raiatea is home to the UNESCO World Heritage Site of Taputapuatea Marae. Explore this ancient ceremonial site, sail along the Faaroa River, and discover the island's rich cultural heritage. Raiatea is also a popular spot for sailing and yachting.

- **Huahine:** Known for its lush vegetation and tranquil ambiance, Huahine is an ideal destination for a relaxing day trip. Visit the island's archaeological sites, explore the sacred blue-eyed eels of Faie, and enjoy the pristine beaches. Huahine's slow pace and natural beauty make it a hidden gem.

GUIDED TOURS AND ACTIVITIES

For a more structured and informative experience, consider joining guided tours and activities that showcase the best of the islands:

- **Lagoon Tours:** Discover the beauty of the lagoons with guided tours that include snorkeling, swimming with sharks and rays, and picnicking on motus. These tours often provide insights into the marine life and local culture, making for an enriching experience.

- **Cultural Tours:** Immerse yourself in Polynesian culture with guided tours that visit traditional villages, ancient marae, and artisan workshops. Learn about the history, customs, and craftsmanship of the islands from knowledgeable guides.

- **Hiking and Nature Tours:** Explore the islands' natural wonders with guided hiking and nature tours. Experienced guides will lead you through lush rainforests, to hidden waterfalls, and up volcanic peaks, providing fascinating information about the flora and fauna.
- **Water Sports and Adventure Tours:** For thrill-seekers, adventure tours offer activities such as jet skiing, scuba diving, kiteboarding, and deep-sea fishing. These tours are led by professionals who ensure safety and provide equipment and instruction.

DIY ADVENTURE TIPS

For those who prefer to explore independently, here are some tips for planning your own day trips and excursions:

- **Research and Plan Ahead:** Before setting out, research the destinations and activities you're interested in. Make note of transportation options, operating hours, and any entry fees. Having a basic itinerary can help you make the most of your day.
- **Rent a Car or Scooter:** Renting a car or scooter gives you the freedom to explore at your own pace. It's a convenient way to visit multiple sites in one day and allows you to venture off the beaten path.

- **Pack Essentials:** Bring along essentials such as water, snacks, sunscreen, and a hat. If you plan to snorkel or swim, pack your gear or rent it from local shops. Don't forget your camera to capture the stunning scenery.
- **Respect Local Guidelines:** When visiting cultural or natural sites, follow any guidelines or regulations in place. Show respect for the environment and local customs to ensure a positive experience for both you and the community.

With these day trips and excursions, you'll have the opportunity to explore the diverse beauty and cultural richness of Tahiti & French Polynesia beyond the main tourist destinations. Up next, we'll delve into the best markets and shops for finding unique souvenirs and local products to bring home.

CHAPTER 12
SHOPPING AND SOUVENIRS
BEST MARKETS AND SHOPS

Tahiti & French Polynesia offer a wealth of shopping opportunities where you can find unique souvenirs, local products, and artisanal crafts. Here are some of the best markets and shops to explore:

- **Papeete Market (Le Marché de Papeete):** Located in the heart of Tahiti's capital, this bustling market is a must-visit for its vibrant atmosphere and diverse offerings. You'll find everything from fresh produce and local delicacies to handmade crafts, jewelry, and traditional pareos (sarongs). It's the perfect place to pick up authentic souvenirs and gifts.

- **Tahiti Pearl Market:** Renowned for its exquisite black pearls, the Tahiti Pearl Market offers a wide selection of pearl jewelry, from elegant necklaces to intricate earrings. The knowledgeable staff can guide you through the process of selecting the perfect pearl, and you can even watch a demonstration of how pearls are harvested.

- **Galerie des Tropiques (Moorea):** This charming gallery on the island of Moorea showcases the work of local artists and artisans. You'll find beautiful paintings, sculptures, and handcrafted items that reflect the natural beauty and cultural heritage of Polynesia. It's an excellent place to find one-of-a-kind pieces for your home or as gifts.

- **Vanilla Valley (Taha'a):** Taha'a is known as the "Vanilla Island," and a visit to Vanilla Valley is a must for those interested in this fragrant spice. Take a tour of the plantation to learn about the cultivation process and purchase high-quality vanilla products, including beans, extracts, and oils.

- **Artisan Markets:** Many islands have local artisan markets where you can find handmade crafts, woven baskets, carved wooden tikis, and shell jewelry. These markets are a great way to support local artisans and bring home unique, culturally significant items.

WHAT TO BUY

Local Products and Handicrafts. When shopping in Tahiti & French Polynesia, keep an eye out for these distinctive local products and handicrafts:

- **Tahitian Black Pearls:** These lustrous pearls are among the most sought-after souvenirs. They come in a range of colors, from deep black to shimmering green and blue.

- **Pareos (Sarongs):** These colorful and versatile garments are a staple of Polynesian fashion. Made from lightweight fabric, pareos can be worn as skirts, dresses, or beach cover-ups. They come in a variety of patterns and designs, often featuring floral motifs and traditional symbols.
- **Monoi Oil:** This fragrant oil is made from coconut oil infused with the petals of Tahitian gardenias (tiare flowers). It is used as a moisturizer, hair conditioner, and massage oil. Monoi oil is a wonderful natural product that captures the essence of the islands.
- **Wood Carvings:** Polynesian wood carvings are known for their intricate designs and cultural significance. Common items include tikis (spiritual figures), bowls, and totems.
- **Tapa Cloth:** This traditional fabric is made from the bark of mulberry trees and decorated with intricate patterns. Tapa cloth can be used as wall hangings, tablecloths, or incorporated into various craft projects.

Shopping Etiquette

When shopping in Tahiti & French Polynesia, keep these etiquette tips in mind:

- **Bargaining: Bargaining** is not a common practice in Tahiti & French Polynesia, especially in established shops and markets. Prices are generally fixed, and it's best to pay the listed price. However, in smaller markets or with individual artisans, you can politely ask if there's any room for negotiation.

- **Supporting Local Artisans:** Whenever possible, buy directly from local artisans and small businesses. These dances are typically performed during festivals, celebrations, and cultural events.
- **Respect for Cultural Items:** Some items, such as tikis and other carvings, hold cultural and spiritual significance. Treat these items with respect and ask the seller about their meaning and proper handling.
- **Cash vs. Cards:** While many shops accept credit and debit cards, it's a good idea to carry some cash, especially in smaller markets and remote areas. Having smaller denominations can be helpful for making purchases.

By exploring the vibrant markets and shops of Tahiti & French Polynesia, you'll find unique souvenirs and local products that capture the spirit and beauty of the islands. Up next, we'll delve into special interests, including honeymoon and romantic getaways, family-friendly activities, solo travel tips, and wellness and spa retreats, to cater to a variety of travel preferences.

CHAPTER 13
SPECIAL INTERESTS
HONEYMOON AND ROMANTIC GETAWAYS

Tahiti & French Polynesia are renowned for their romantic ambiance, making them ideal destinations for honeymooners and couples seeking an intimate escape. Here are some top recommendations for a romantic getaway:

- **Private Overwater Bungalows:** Nothing says romance like an overwater bungalow. Resorts such as the Four Seasons Bora Bora and the Conrad Bora Bora Nui offer luxurious bungalows with private plunge pools, direct lagoon access, and stunning sunset views. Enjoy breakfast delivered by canoe and candlelit dinners on your private deck.

- **Couples' Spa Treatments:** Indulge in a relaxing spa day with your partner. Many resorts offer couples' spa packages that include massages, facials, and traditional Polynesian treatments using locally sourced ingredients like coconut oil and Tahitian vanilla.

- **Sunset Cruises:** Experience the magic of a Tahitian sunset with a private sunset cruise. Sail through the serene lagoons of Bora Bora or Moorea, sip on champagne, and watch as the sun dips below the horizon, painting the sky in shades of pink and orange.

- **Private Beach Picnics:** Arrange for a secluded beach picnic on a pristine motu. Enjoy a gourmet meal, swim in crystal-clear waters, and bask in the tranquility of your private paradise. Many resorts offer personalized picnic packages for couples.
- **Starlit Dinners:** Dine under the stars with a starlit dinner on the beach. Enjoy a gourmet meal prepared by a private chef, surrounded by the soft glow of lanterns and the sound of gentle waves. It's a truly unforgettable experience for couples.

FAMILY-FRIENDLY ACTIVITIES

Tahiti & French Polynesia are also great destinations for families, offering a wide range of activities that cater to all ages:

- **Lagoon Excursions:** Families can enjoy fun-filled days exploring the lagoons. Activities such as snorkeling, paddleboarding, and swimming with rays and sharks are sure to delight children and adults alike. Many tour operators offer family-friendly excursions with safety equipment and experienced guides.
- **Cultural Workshops:** Engage in hands-on cultural workshops where families can learn about Polynesian

traditions. Try your hand at making flower crowns, weaving palm fronds, or learning traditional dance moves. Ensure you pack sufficient water and snacks for your journey.

- **Nature Hikes:** Explore the natural beauty of the islands with family-friendly hikes. Trails such as the Opunohu Valley in Moorea and the Fautaua Valley in Tahiti offer stunning scenery and opportunities to spot local wildlife. These cherished memories will stay with you long after your trip has ended.
- **Aquariums and Wildlife Centers:** Visit local aquariums and wildlife centers to learn about the marine life and ecosystems of French Polynesia. The Moorea Dolphin Center and the Bora Bora Lagoonarium are popular attractions that offer educational programs and interactive experiences.
- **Beach Days:** Spend relaxing days on the beautiful beaches, building sandcastles, swimming in the warm waters, and enjoying picnics. Many beaches have calm, shallow areas that are perfect for young children.

SOLO TRAVEL TIPS

Solo travelers will find plenty to see and do in Tahiti & French Polynesia, with opportunities for adventure, relaxation, and cultural exploration:

- **Join Group Tours:** Joining group tours and excursions is a great way to meet other travelers and enjoy guided experiences. Whether it's a snorkeling tour, a cultural workshop, or a hiking expedition, group activities offer camaraderie and safety.
- **Stay in Hostels or Guesthouses:** Opt for hostels or guesthouses where you can connect with fellow travelers. These accommodations often have communal areas where guests can socialize, share travel tips, and plan outings together.
- **Embrace Solo Activities:** Enjoy the freedom of solo travel by engaging in activities that interest you. Take a yoga class on the beach, rent a bike to explore the island, or spend a day relaxing at a spa. Solo travel allows you to tailor your itinerary to your preferences
- **Connect with Locals:** Don't hesitate to strike up conversations with locals. The people of Tahiti & French Polynesia are known for their warm hospitality and are often happy to share insights about their culture and recommendations for hidden gems.
- **Stay Safe:** While the islands are generally safe, it's important to take common-sense precautions. Keep your belongings secure, stay aware of your surroundings, and

avoid isolated areas after dark. Let someone know your plans if you venture off on your own.

WELLNESS AND SPA RETREATS

For those seeking relaxation and rejuvenation, Tahiti & French Polynesia offer a range of wellness and spa retreats that promote holistic well-being:

- **Yoga and Meditation Retreats:** Join a yoga and meditation retreat in a serene tropical setting. Many resorts and wellness centers offer retreats that combine daily yoga sessions, meditation practices, and healthy meals. These retreats provide a peaceful escape and a chance to reconnect with yourself.
- **Thalassotherapy:** Experience the healing benefits of thalassotherapy, which uses seawater and marine products for therapeutic treatments. The InterContinental Bora Bora Resort & Thalasso Spa offers a range of thalassotherapy treatments, including hydrotherapy baths, seaweed wraps, and marine facials.
- **Traditional Polynesian Massages:** Treat yourself to a traditional Polynesian massage, known as taurumi. This therapeutic practice combines deep tissue massage with rhythmic movements and the use of natural oils. It's a deeply relaxing and rejuvenating experience.

- **Detox Programs:** Participate in a detox program that includes healthy meals, juice cleanses, and wellness activities. These programs are designed to cleanse the body, boost energy, and promote overall well-being. Many wellness resorts offer tailored detox packages.
- **Mindfulness and Wellness Workshops:** Engage in mindfulness and wellness workshops that focus on holistic health. Learn techniques for stress reduction, healthy living, and self-care practices. These workshops provide valuable tools for maintaining wellness beyond your vacation.

Whether you're seeking a romantic escape, a family adventure, solo exploration, or a wellness retreat, Tahiti & French Polynesia offer diverse experiences to cater to every traveler's interests. Up next, we'll conclude with some final travel tips, staying connected, and planning your return trip to ensure your journey is as memorable as possible.

CHAPTER 14
FINAL TRAVEL TIPS

As you prepare to conclude your unforgettable journey through Tahiti & French Polynesia, here are some final travel tips to ensure a smooth and memorable experience:

- **Stay Flexible:** Embrace the island lifestyle and stay flexible with your plans. Weather conditions and unexpected events can sometimes alter your itinerary, but these moments often lead to unexpected adventures and discoveries.
- **Document Your Memories:** Capture the beauty of the islands through photographs and videos. Keep a travel journal to document your experiences, thoughts, and emotions. These memories will be cherished long after your trip.
- **Learn a Few Local Phrases:** While English is widely spoken, learning a few basic Tahitian or French phrases can enhance your interactions with locals and show your appreciation for their culture.
- **Respect Local Customs:** Show respect for local customs and traditions by dressing modestly, asking permission before taking photos, and being mindful of your behavior at cultural sites.

- **Stay Connected:** Share your travel experiences with friends and family through social media, blogs, or personal messages. Staying connected allows you to relive your journey and inspire others to explore Tahiti & French Polynesia.

STAYING CONNECTED AND KEEPING MEMORIES

In the age of technology, staying connected and preserving your travel memories is easier than ever. Here are some tips to help you stay connected and keep your memories alive:

- **Social Media:** Share your travel experiences on social media platforms like Instagram, Facebook, and Twitter. Use hashtags related to Tahiti & French Polynesia to connect with other travelers and discover new places to visit.
- **Travel Blogs:** Consider starting a travel blog to document your journey in detail. Share your stories, tips, and photos to create a personal travel diary that others can enjoy and benefit from.
- **Photo Books:** Create a photo book or scrapbook of your trip. Print your favorite photos and add captions, ticket stubs, and other mementos to create a tangible keepsake of your adventure.

- **Video Diaries:** Record video diaries of your experiences, thoughts, and impressions throughout your trip. Edit these videos into a travel vlog that you can watch and share with others.
- **Digital Storage:** Back up your photos and videos on cloud storage platforms like Google Drive, Dropbox, or iCloud. This ensures your memories are safely stored and easily accessible.

PLAN YOUR RETURN TRIP

Once you've experienced the magic of Tahiti & French Polynesia, you'll likely be eager to return. Here are some tips for planning your next adventure:

- **Explore New Islands:** Consider visiting different islands on your next trip. Each island offers unique experiences, landscapes, and activities, so there's always something new to discover.
- **Time Your Visit:** Plan your return trip around specific events or festivals, such as Heiva i Tahiti or the Billabong Pro Tahiti. These events add an extra layer of excitement and cultural immersion to your journey.
- **Reconnect with Locals:** Stay in touch with local friends and contacts you've made during your trip. They can

provide valuable insights and recommendations for your next visit.

- **Try New Activities:** Make a list of activities and attractions you missed during your first trip and prioritize them for your return. Whether it's diving in new locations, hiking different trails, or exploring additional cultural sites, there's always more to experience.

- **Reflect and Plan:** Reflect on your experiences and what you enjoyed most about your trip. Use these insights to plan a personalized itinerary that aligns with your interests and preferences.

Tahiti & French Polynesia are destinations that captivate the heart and soul. Whether you're drawn to the stunning landscapes, rich cultural heritage, or warm hospitality, there's no doubt that your journey here will leave a lasting impression. With this comprehensive travel guide, you're well-equipped to make the most of your visit and create memories that will last a lifetime.

CHAPTER 15
PREPARING FOR YOUR TRIP
PRE-TRIP PLANNING AND RESEARCH

Proper planning and research are key to a successful and enjoyable trip to Tahiti & French Polynesia. Here are some essential steps to take before you embark on your journey:

- **Research Destinations:** Study the various islands and choose the ones that align with your interests and preferences. Consider factors such as activities, attractions, accommodation options, and travel logistics.

- **Create an Itinerary:** Outline a flexible itinerary that includes your planned activities, accommodation details, and transportation arrangements. Include buffer days for relaxation and unexpected adventures.

- **Book Accommodations and Flights:** Make reservations for your flights, accommodations, and any tours or activities in advance. This ensures availability and often secures better rates.

- **Check Travel Documents:** Ensure your passport is valid for at least six months beyond your planned departure date. Check if you need a visa or any other travel documents for entry into French Polynesia.

Health and Safety Precautions: Schedule a visit to your healthcare provider to discuss any necessary vaccinations or health precautions. Purchase travel insurance that covers medical expenses, emergency evacuation, and trip cancellations.

BUDGETING AND FINANCIAL PLANNING

Creating a budget for your trip helps you manage expenses and enjoy a worry-free vacation. Here are some tips for effective budgeting:

- **Estimate Costs:** Calculate the estimated costs of flights, accommodations, meals, transportation, activities, and souvenirs. Consider using a budgeting app or spreadsheet to keep track of your expenses.
- **Set a Daily Budget:** Determine a daily spending limit for meals, activities, and other expenses. This helps you stay within your overall budget and avoid overspending.
- **Prepare for Miscellaneous Expenses:** Set aside a portion of your budget for unexpected expenses, such as emergencies, additional activities, or last-minute purchases.
- **Currency Exchange:** Research currency exchange rates and fees. Consider exchanging a small amount of money before you arrive for immediate expenses, and use ATMs for additional cash withdrawals.

Travel Insurance and Health Precautions

Travel insurance and health precautions are essential components of a safe and secure trip:

- **Purchase Travel Insurance:** Choose a comprehensive travel insurance plan that covers medical expenses, emergency evacuation, trip cancellations, and lost or stolen belongings. Review the policy details to understand coverage limits and exclusions.
- **Pack a First Aid Kit:** Include basic medical supplies such as band-aids, pain relievers, antiseptic wipes, and any prescription medications. Consider packing motion sickness tablets if you plan to take boat trips.
- **Stay Hydrated and Sun-Safe:** The tropical climate can lead to dehydration and sunburn. Drink plenty of water, use sunscreen with high SPF, and wear protective clothing and a hat.
- **Practice Good Hygiene:** Wash your hands regularly, use hand sanitizer, and follow food safety guidelines to avoid stomach illnesses. Be cautious with tap water and opt for bottled or filtered water when necessary.

Cultural Sensitivity and Responsible Travel

Being culturally sensitive and practicing responsible travel ensures a positive experience for both you and the local community:

- **Learn About Local Customs:** Familiarize yourself with the cultural norms and traditions of Tahiti & French Polynesia. Show respect for local customs, dress modestly when visiting cultural sites, and use basic Tahitian or French phrases.
- **Support Sustainable Tourism:** Choose eco-friendly accommodations and activities that prioritize sustainability. Participate in community-based tourism initiatives that benefit local residents and preserve the environment.
- **Minimize Environmental Impact:** Follow Leave No Trace principles by disposing of waste properly, avoiding single-use plastics, and respecting wildlife and natural habitats.
- **Engage with the Community:** Take the time to connect with locals, learn about their way of life, and support local businesses. Be open to new experiences and show appreciation for the hospitality you receive.

TECHNOLOGY AND CONNECTIVITY

Staying connected during your trip helps you navigate, communicate, and share your experiences:

- **Travel Apps:** Download travel apps that can assist with navigation, language translation, currency conversion, and itinerary management. Popular apps include Google Maps, Duolingo, XE Currency, and TripIt.
- **Roaming Plans and SIM Cards:** Check with your mobile carrier about international roaming plans or consider purchasing a local SIM card for more affordable data and call rates. Ensure your phone is unlocked before traveling.
- **Emergency Contacts:** Keep a list of important contacts, including local emergency numbers, your country's embassy or consulate, and your travel insurance provider. Share your travel plans with a trusted friend or family member.
- **Backup Your Data:** Regularly back up your photos, videos, and important documents to cloud storage or an external drive. This ensures you don't lose valuable memories or essential information in case of device loss or damage.

By thoroughly preparing for your trip, budgeting effectively, practicing cultural sensitivity, and staying connected, you can ensure a smooth and memorable journey to Tahiti & French Polynesia. This comprehensive guide has covered everything you need to know, making you well-equipped to embark on an unforgettable adventure in this tropical paradise.

CONCLUSION

As we conclude this comprehensive guide to Tahiti & French Polynesia Travel Guide 2025-2026, we hope you feel equipped and inspired to embark on the journey of a lifetime. From the serene beaches of Bora Bora to the lush valleys of Moorea, and the vibrant culture of Tahiti, these islands offer a magical experience that captivates the heart and soul.

Throughout this guide, we've explored every facet of what makes Tahiti & French Polynesia such a unique and enchanting destination. We've provided detailed information on how to get there, where to stay, and the must-see attractions that await you. We've delved into the rich culinary delights, vibrant cultural heritage, and the countless adventures that the islands have to offer. From the luxurious overwater bungalows to the traditional Polynesian cuisine and the fascinating history, there's something for every traveler to discover and cherish.

We trust that this guide has served as a valuable resource, offering insights, tips, and recommendations to help you make the most of your visit. Whether you're a first-time visitor or returning to explore new horizons, Tahiti & French Polynesia promise an unforgettable experience that will leave you with lasting memories and a longing to return.

As you prepare for your journey, we encourage you to take with you the spirit of exploration, respect for the local culture, and a commitment to sustainable travel. By doing so, you will not only enrich your own experience but also contribute to the preservation and appreciation of these beautiful islands for future generations.

Thank you for choosing Tahiti & French Polynesia Travel Guide 2025-2026 as your trusted companion. We are grateful for the opportunity to guide you through this paradise on Earth. We hope you have a wonderful trip filled with adventure, relaxation, and meaningful connections.

We'd love to hear about your experiences and feedback. Please consider leaving a review of this guide to help other travelers and let us know how we can continue to improve. Your insights are invaluable and greatly appreciated.

Safe travels, and may your journey be as extraordinary as the islands themselves.

Isabelle M. Fry

BONUS
TRAVEL PLANNER

TRAVEL PLANNER

7 DAY TRIP

Day 1:
→
→
→

Day 2:
→
→
→

Day 3:
→
→
→

Day 4:
→
→
→

Tahiti & French Polynesia Travel Guide 2025-2026

TRAVEL PLANNER

7 DAY TRIP

Day 5:
→
→
→

Day 6:
→
→
→

Day 7:
→
→
→

Final Note:
→
→
→

Isabelle M. Fry

TRAVEL BUDGET PLANNER

Travel budget *PLANNER*

DESTINATION				TRAVEL DATES			

PRE-TRIP EXPENSES

expenses	budget	actual
TOTAL:		

TRANSPORTATION

expenses	budget	actual
TOTAL:		

ACCOMMODATION

expenses	budget	actual
TOTAL:		

ACTIVITIES

expenses	budget	actual
TOTAL:		

FOOD & DRINK

expenses	budget	actual
TOTAL:		

OTHER

expenses	budget	actual
TOTAL:		

GRAND TOTAL	budget	actual

NOTES

Tahiti & French Polynesia Travel Guide 2025-2026

NOTEPAD

date   /   NOTES

Printed in Dunstable, United Kingdom